WREATH — Christmas Card

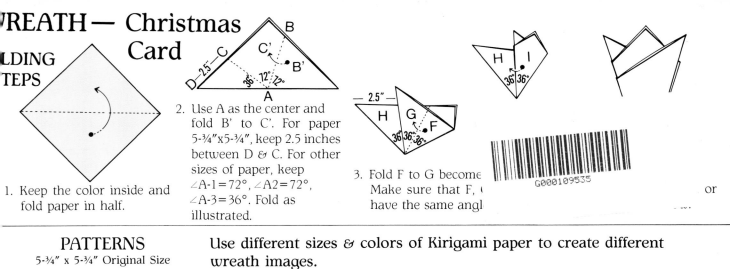

FOLDING STEPS

1. Keep the color inside and fold paper in half.

2. Use A as the center and fold B' to C'. For paper 5-¾"x5-¾", keep 2.5 inches between D & C. For other sizes of paper, keep ∠A-1=72°, ∠A2=72°, ∠A-3=36°. Fold as illustrated.

3. Fold F to G become Make sure that F, have the same ang

G000109535

PATTERNS
5-¾" x 5-¾" Original Size

Use different sizes & colors of Kirigami paper to create different wreath images.

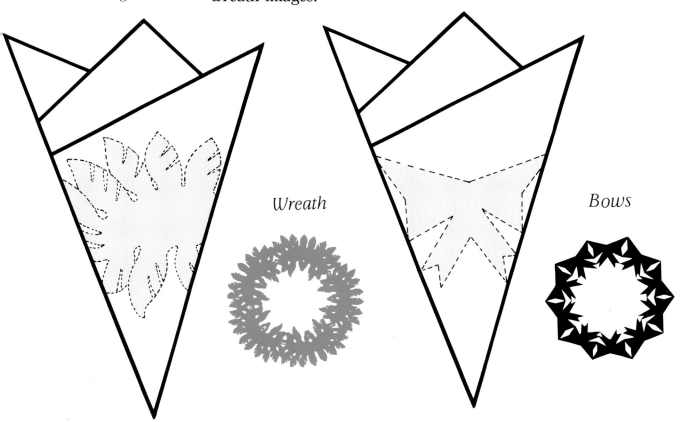

Wreath

Bows

3

4

SNOW FLAKES — Window Decorations

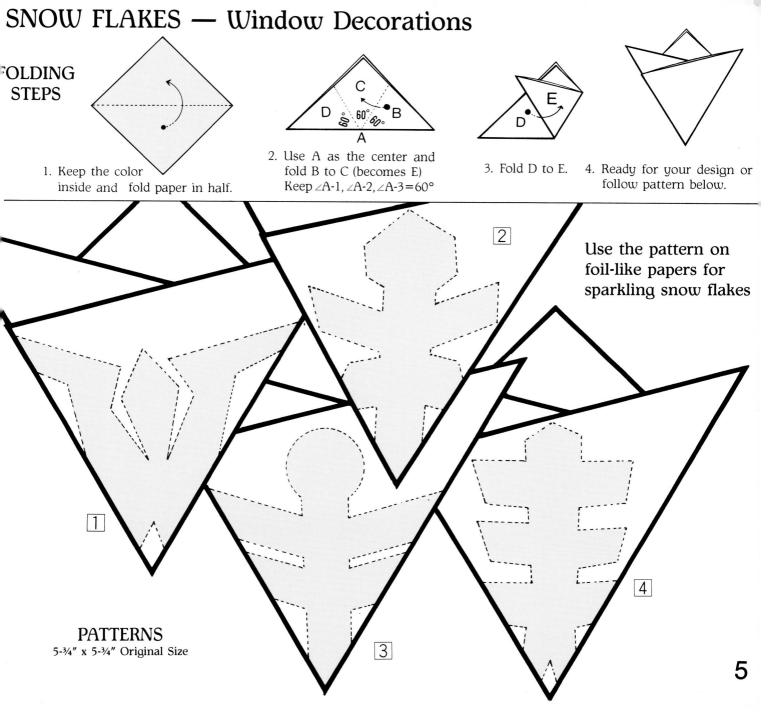

FOLDING STEPS

1. Keep the color inside and fold paper in half.

2. Use A as the center and fold B to C (becomes E) Keep ∠A-1, ∠A-2, ∠A-3=60°

3. Fold D to E.

4. Ready for your design or follow pattern below.

Use the pattern on foil-like papers for sparkling snow flakes

1

2

3

4

PATTERNS
5-¾" x 5-¾" Original Size

5

6

TAR — Gift Wrapping

FOLDING STEPS

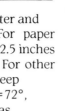

1. Keep the color inside and fold paper in half.

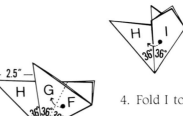

2. Use A as the center and fold B' to C'. For paper 5-¾"x5-¾", keep 2.5 inches between D & C. For other sizes of paper, keep ∠A-1=72°, ∠A2=72°, ∠A-3=36°. Fold as illustrated.

3. Fold F to G becomes I. Make sure that F, G & H have the same angle (36°)

4. Fold I to H.

5. Ready for your design or follow pattern below.

PATTERNS
5-¾" x 5-¾" Original Size

Coordinate different colors of Kirigami paper with your wrapping paper.

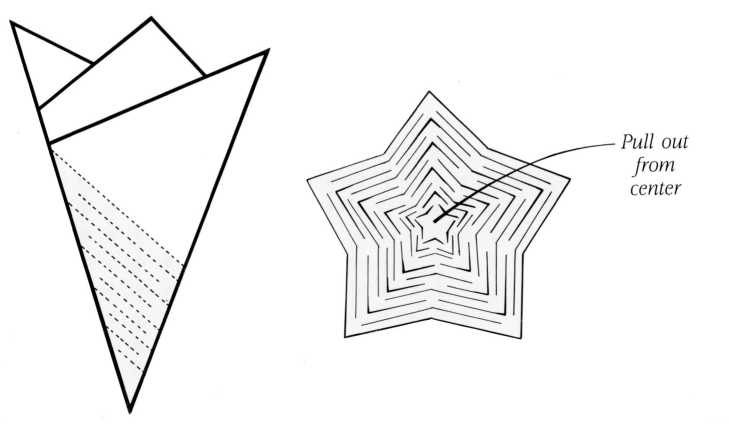

Pull out from center

7

8   *See page 14 for pattern.*

CHRISTMAS TREE COLLECTION

Earrings • Party Name Tags • Christmas Trees • Gift Wrapping • Tree Ornaments

Christmas Ornament

FOLDING STEPS

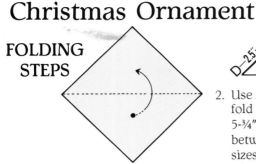

1. Keep the color inside and fold paper in half.

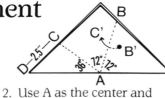

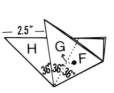

2. Use A as the center and fold B' to C'. For paper 5-¾"x5-¾", keep 2.5 inches between D & C. For other sizes of paper, keep ∠A-1=72°, ∠A2=72°, ∠A-3=36°. Fold as illustrated.

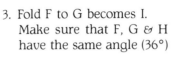

3. Fold F to G becomes I. Make sure that F, G & H have the same angle (36°)

4. Fold I to H.

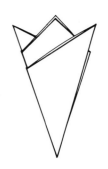

5. Ready for your design follow pattern below.

PATTERNS
5-¾" x 5-¾" Original Size

Decorate with jingle bells for maximum effect.

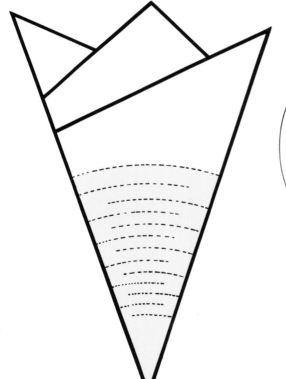

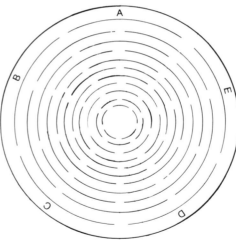

❶ *Pull points A, B, C, D, E together and glue.*

❷ *Attach bow and string.*

10

Tree-top Ornament

FOLDING STEPS

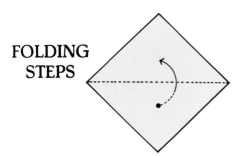

1. Keep the color inside and fold paper in half.

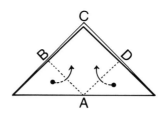

2. Using A,B&D as centers, fold both to C (half fold AB and AD).

3. Fold in half.

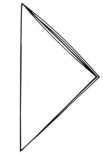

4. Ready for your design or follow pattern below.

PATTERNS
5-¾" x 5-¾" Original Size

Pattern may also be used for gift wrapping.

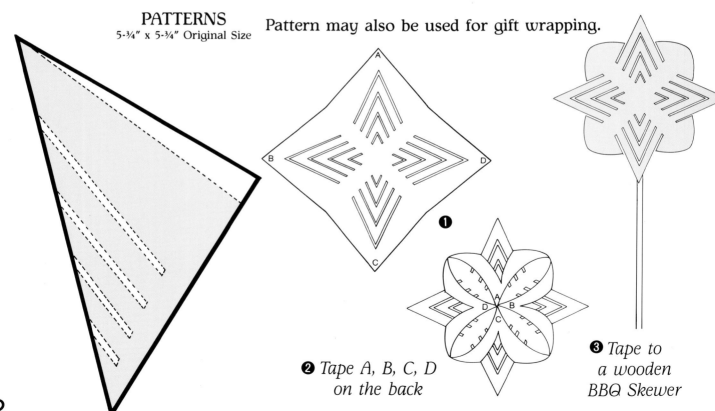

❶

❷ *Tape A, B, C, D on the back*

❸ *Tape to a wooden BBQ Skewer*

12

CHRISTMAS TREE

Use green wrapping paper for a larger Christmas tree.

FOLDING STEPS

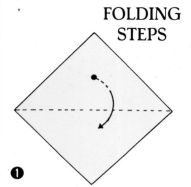

❶ For this project, please keep the <u>color outside</u> and fold paper in half.

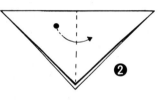

❷

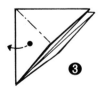

❸

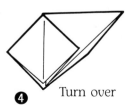

❹ Turn over

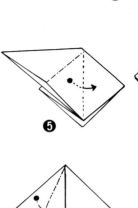

❺

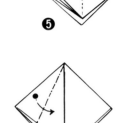

❻

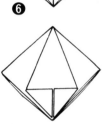

❼ Turn over

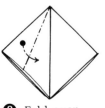

❽ Fold over

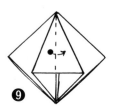

❾

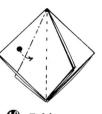

❿ Fold over

⓫ Do the same on other side

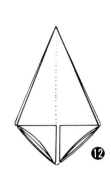

⓬

PATTERNS
5-¾" x 5-¾" Original Size

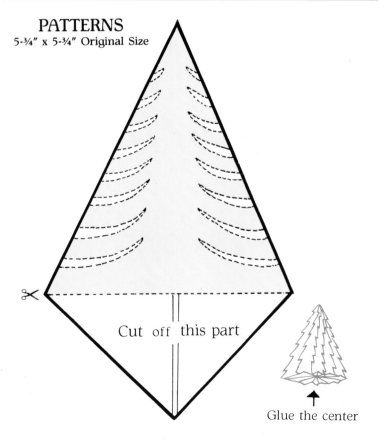

✂

Cut off this part

Glue the center